Docker

Advanced Strategies for Taking Control of Docker Programming

Miles Price

Table of Contents

Introduction..1

Chapter One: Docker Containers 3

Chapter Two: Images with Docker 15

Chapter Three: The Docker Orchestration 25

Chapter Four: Managing Swarms...........................29

Chapter Five: Networking.......................................33

Chapter Six: Building a Web Server.......................37

Chapter Seven: Setting Nodes. Js 40

Chapter Eight: Mongo DB..43

Chapter Nine: Setting Up Docker NGINX 47

Chapter Ten: Setting Up an ASP. Net....................50

Chapter Eleven: Kubernetecs Architecture 54

Chapter Twelve: Cluster Deployment.....................58

Conclusion 74

Additionally, the information in the following pages is intended only for informational purposes and should thus be thought of as universal. As befitting its nature, it is presented without assurance regarding its prolonged validity or interim quality. Trademarks that are mentioned are done without written consent and can in no way be considered an endorsement from the trademark holder.

Introduction

Congratulations on downloading *Docker* and thank you for doing so.

The following chapters will discuss the various strategies that you can use Docker so that you can take the knowledge that you already possess and advance it to the next level to impress your friends and your employers.

Before you start reading this book, it is vital that you already have knowledge of how Docker works and the basics of Docker so that you can better understand the code that you will see in this book.

Do not let the code that you see scare you away from Docker. Make sure to take your coding one step at a time or else you may end up messing up and not getting the result that you want. There may be times when you use the wrong code but get the result that you desire, however, it is not going to happen often. Therefore, you should not get used to it happening.

If you have not already, pick up the beginner's book for this Docker series! *Docker: The Comprehensive Beginner's Guide to Take Control of Docker Programming.*

Docker

Do not forget to pick up the tips and tricks book so that you can learn some useful and fun things to do with Docker. *Docker: Tips and Tricks to Accelerate Your Learning*

There are plenty of books on this subject on the market, thanks again for choosing this one! Every effort was made to ensure it is full of as much useful information as possible, please enjoy!

Chapter One:

Docker Containers

Thinking about containers in a computer program is an abstract idea. However, the containers in Docker will run on a function that will set the resources that are needed so that you have access to them. The resources in the container will typically be physical such as a computer processor or the network the computer is using. These functions can be applied to complete mathematical equations or other complex tasks such as the creation of an application that will operate across several machines at the same time.

During the resources lifespan, they will become more powerful since the application will not be using all of the power that the machine offers. So, the resources will be important when it comes to achieving goals by helping with how the computer works as a whole. The resources will work with the computer's hardware that will run concurrently so that the fractions can be utilized from the physical resources.

There are various techniques that you will use for the simulations which will be known as virtualizations. But, a lot of users believe that machines that use virtualization will work in a virtual environment. However, this is only one of the aspects of it. The memory for a machine will be virtual and will be used by the operating system and the general steps that will be followed so that the computer can keep going for the application to be saved on the computer's memory. The computer's memory will be a space that is dedicated to every application on the computer as long as it does not use more RAM than what the computer has to offer.

Containers are another part of the computer's aspect for virtualization since they sometimes referred to as the operating system virtualization. A container that is used on a Linux system will make it seem like the computer is isolated; which in turn makes it appear as if it is running on its own operating system so the application that is being used can continue to be used. You need to look to the local disk so that you can see if it is prepared for the file that will be placed on it.

A computer's memory will hold files and any other piece of data that a file needs; this will include the operating system after it has been freshly booted. Should you be ready to reboot your operating system, then you will need to use the host so that you can create a container.

The first step is to look at the namespace so that you can make sure that it is isolated. The namespaces that are isolated will contain all of the resources that are needed for the application. Whenever the namespace is isolated, it will enable the host to examine each container individually as well as the resources that are in the container to see how they will be seen by the standard user such as yourself.

Because you will be working off a restricted view for the namespace, the container is not going to have access to any file that it does not need to access to. This will include the virtualizations, no matter where the permissions fall. At this point in time, the virtualization cannot be seen because it will not have the option of listing the permissions or interacting with any application that is not already inside the container.

Therefore, to maximize how efficient files are, the ones on the operating system and the directories, they will end up being shared between several different containers that hold the same namespace as the containers that came before it. Applications will have the option of making a change to the container; but only if they are allowed to modify the file that is already on the system, or they are trying to create a new one. The new files that are created will host a new operating system. Any changes will only be changed on the inside of the copy so that it can be written inside Docker.

The parts of the container that are shared will make it to where there are several containers – all on a single host – which causes them to work together more efficiently. When it comes to looking at how the host controls the resources that are used by the container, you will notice that the resources are governed on a similar bandwidth for the network so that the container gets all of the resources that it needs without any other application being impacted.

For example, say you have a container that has been constructed so that it cannot use more than ten percent of the computer's CPU. So, if there is an application that tries to run, but it does not have access to the rest of the CPU. The Linux system will end up governing the technology with a strategy that is called cgroups.

The resources being governed will not be required in every case for the containers that are located on the same host. All of these containers will appear to be cooperative will allow the operating system to be dynamic in the assignment of any resources. The system will ultimately end up adapting to the change for the code to run properly.

The automatic startup will be based on the virtualization for the operating system as well as the execution of the namespace. The isolation of the namespace along with the resources that are being used for the development and testing of the application will also play a part in the startup as well.

As you examine the development process, the developers are allowed to iterate quickly because of the resources and the environment that is being used throughout the system. The applications that have been containerized are only going to work with the system that the developer is working on so that they can be similar to the production system.

The instant start and a variety of smaller footprints will end up adding a few benefits on the cloud and the applications so that they can be set to scale quickly depending on the application that is running. The instances will need to fit on the machine for all the resources to be maximized.

Complex containers

When it comes to running a web service, you will have the option to use Docker to compose a farm of web servers that will run a HAProxy load balancer. Docker developers are making it their mission to create a tool that will be available on ARM; which is why Composer was made in the first place. The Composer binary will be allowed to run on a Raspberry Pi board which will open up a new world for those that use Pi.

Installing

Your Docker Composer has to be installed from Raspberry Pi which you can locate it on this website. https://github.com/hypriot/compose

Docker compose

If you want a container to be set up with a specific set of containers, you will need to compose a YML file. After you have done that, you will possess three containers that will be based on the application image for the first container that was built with the HAProxy.

For each web application, there will be a host of servers that will have a port exposed. The HAProxy will have access to the port because of the application and its interface.

Docker

HAProxy

The HAProxy has to be configured before it can be mapped to the container. You may see a file that is similar to the example below.

Example

Worldwide

List 721.1.1.0 note 1

List 721.1.1.0 note1 alert

Set

List worldwide

Hold HTTP

Change 'HTTP list'

Change do list void

Overdone tied 4000

Overdone customer 5000

Overdone server 90000

Hear statistics: 80

Statistics turned on

Statistics Uri /

Beginning balanced

tied 1.1.1.1: 90

mode HTTP

start_ ending_ aj_ endings

ending_ aj_ endings

mode HTTP

...

Your HAProxy will check to determine how health the server is that you are using for it to figure out if any web applications will end up running into problems. By knowing if there are issues you may encounter you will be better equipped to fix them before they get to the point where you cannot fix it which will force you to scrape the code and start over.

Running a web server farm

Once everything has been set up, you will utilize the containers by spinning them so that you can compose a function that will allow you to interact with the functions and options of the program. When you decide to use the proper function, all of your containers will start at the same time that your background server starts.

While an applications server spins, you will notice that there will be an instance that is used by the HAProxy. Inside this container, you will have access to any requests that are filtered through the container to balance the servers and the HAProxy. Every log and container will be running at the same time whenever the correct command is inserted into the command prompt.

The curl action will be used for you to test the application as a whole on your server farm.

Container names will make an enormous difference depending on the request that you have placed in the program. There will be a fourth container that will hold the same name as the first one in the sequence of containers. The HAProxy will end up examining every request in a round robin fashion so that the servers can be enabled to handle a third of the load that is bouncing between the servers being used.

Packaging a container, so it is ready for deployment

A container's platform will hold an SDN (software-defined networking) for any applications that are being used. This allows multiple containers to be developed through several hosts. The SDN will make sure that the containers are distributed properly so they can communicate with each other, even if they have been relocated.

Platforms can be enhanced so that you use three tools to help with the core orchestration: swarm, compose, and machine. Each feature will be added along with the intelligence that will be used to help you deal with any application that is being spread across several containers.

A system will be put in place when it comes to packaging your code before it is deployed. This will come from having a few different distributions instead of having the usual ones that you always see on the Linux system. But, each system will use the same kernel. Once you have realized that containers occupy a space that falls between development and the operations process, the code used will give way for the developers to test the quality assurance of their code before it is produced.

Various parts of the Linux system can be used by the applications that you do not find inside of the kernel. These packages will be easier to find despite the environment that they are running on.

After the code has been tested to make sure that the packages are performing properly, the package will be deployed to the user to be used in their code.

If an error message appears in the code, the quality assurance team will catch it. However, since the developers are human, there are a few errors that slip through the cracks. If you find an error or any other problem with the Docker code, you need to report it to the development team so that the program can be updated for it to be more efficient for its users.

COMPLEX

Container management challenges

To realize the full potential of all the benefits that Docker provides you, you will have to realize that they come in the forms of challenges that you have to find a solution to. Here are a few challenges that you will face when you are managing containers with Docker.

1. Disconnected release cycle/ fragmented process: so that your transitions are smoother, it is important that you know when new things are released in Docker, they are

released at the same time. So, if they are not released at the same time, then the process will be considered fragmented, and there will be several parts of the program that are not going to work until they have everything they need to run properly.

2. Lack of control: developers are working to find a service that allows them to work quickly so that they can create, test, and deploy applications. While this is happening, the operations team will work on controlling and governing the applications so that they can try and prevent containers from sprawling. If a container is sprawling, it can cause an increase in infrastructure costs and resource overconsumption. If there is not a way for you to govern your containers, then they will end up running out of control, and the containers will no longer be a valuable resource for Docker users.

3. Unique monitoring requirements: Docker's environment will require several special capabilities for monitoring. Take, for example, the API level integration with Docker and the instrumentation that has been built into the images that are used with Docker. The requirements will go beyond the usual monitoring requirements.

4. Container scaling: containers are complex, but they are a vital part of the Docker program. Not only that, but they are used for the deployment of applications across Docker and other infrastructures. But, it will require a delicate orchestration of deployments and the management of run times.

5. Vulnerability protection and compliance: being that Docker includes several parts of the operating system. Docker containers can be used to incorporate vulnerabilities such as ghost. By protecting the Docker environment, you will be required security at the host level where containers and images are being used. By updating an immutable container, you will be creating an entirely new management system.

Best practices for container management

The better that you control the containers you use, the easier it will be for you to use Docker. However, management is always easier said than done. Here, you will learn some of the best management practices for your containers.

1. Combine speed with control: the cloud lifecycle management will address governance and self-service. With this solution, you will not only get a self-service catalog that the developers can request a new Docker infrastructure such as a Docker swarm with a single click. This catalog will make it easier for developers to identify and choose an image quickly; therefore, it will save time because you will not need to build an image.

2. Streamline orchestration and governance of container infrastructures: there is a new Docker-based cloud application that will integrate applications and

middleware that is running on a virtualized system. Cloud management will allow IT operations to be deployed and managed in a hybrid environment that contains specific policies. These policies will be put in places for different workload types that are out there. The deamons for a digital enterprise will be called a new suite of cloud-native and micro service applications that need to be defined, orchestrated, managed, and governed.

3. Coordinate the continuous integration and continuous delivery pipeline: the release management will be used in governing a lifecycle for a Docker image through all of its stages. But, it will also assist in coordinating the application through the updates by managing several release teams throughout various environments.

4. Provide security across the full stack: vulnerability testing for a container will be done by a blade logic server automation tools. This will end up performing security contained automation protocols through the testing of Docker images so that they can make sure that the containers are not suffering from a critical security vulnerability.

Chapter Two:

Images with Docker

Containers for layers and images

There are a few features that Docker offers users so that they can be used when an image is being built.

1. Process isolation

2. Tooling/ CLI

3. Security

4. Resource management

Process isolation and resource management will be put to use by the Linux system. There are a few security features that you may notice inside of the resource management along with the process isolation; but, here is where your security measures can be found in the SELinux. The SELinux will be different and set apart from your Docker program. There are a few tools that Linux will provide so that you can use them to build an image.

The important thing that you will use when building an image is the image content management and the layering tool. The layering tool contains a technique that will be used when working with images or any content so that you can add abstract feeling to it once they have been built in the container and are being used by the application. The image will provide the foundation that is needed for the container you will be working with. Several other new tools will provide you with the foundation along with the containers that are needed to combine them with other entities.

Your Docker program will have the option to build an image by using a Docker file. This will be a file that can be used as your base image that you want to build on. The instruction can be found in the image's registry that you use most often.

Any extra layers that you use in Docker can be created by using a direct that is placed inside of the Docker file. The run function can be used when you are running a command to manipulate an image. There are some extra packages that you will have the opportunity to install by using this function; this will include Linux package installation tools. The tool will be found in Linux and will be labeled as Hat.

Any other code or content that you will use to create a layer will be done by using the add function from a Docker directory or a URL. Once you have added all of your layers to the foundation, then the application can be made more specific in the creation of the image and how it will be used later on.

Three approaches

When it comes to building an image in Docker, you will have three ways that you can choose from. But, there will be things that you will want to take into consideration so that you can pick the best approach for you.

1. The web server

2. Website content

3. The base image.

As the administrator, you have to build your images by using one of these methods.

1. Interactively which will require you to launch a shell for BASH under the Yum install

2. Creating a Docker file so that you can build on an image with the website you are interacting with.

When you are using the first method, you will be using a CLI so that you can lay down the first image on the web server before you begin creating the image that you will reuse later.

The other option will require that you use a Docker file that contains a fedora image so that it can be installed through a package by using Apache. This all has to be done before the image content is added. Once that is done, the website will be able to be created in a single build.

Option one

The image functions that you use while working with the interactive method will be known as the Fedora function. This ultimately means that you will be working with a public registry that is created specifically for Docker. You will find that this is similar to when you are trying to locate something in a library. The more information that you have about the image that you want to find. The extra information on the image is going to make it to where you can find more options that you might not have considered previously.

When a container is working with an interactive builder, you will be required to run a shell that will be interactive so that Docker can be enabled to run the project's host.

Syntax

Docker execute -l – m fedora party

By using this code, you will be telling Fedora to open the container for the party shell to run. This will occur inside of a container as long as you can locate the Yum commands for the latest updates and ensure that Apache has been installed on your operating system.

After you have finished everything, there should be two Fedora functions that are ready for you to use.

As an admin, you may notice that you see a lot of new images inside the web server. And, as the administrator, you can build a Docker file that will revolve around the image so that the proper file can be added. However, by depending on the path, the content that you use will need to be added to your container after it has been unzipped so that the source is placed directly in the directory.

This is where you will need to create an index that will also be added to the directory that you are using. The file that you use in the end will be the template that you set up so other sites can be built off of it. You will find that it is easier on you because you will not be building from the ground up each time that you create a website.

Docker consists of commands that will end up being what determines which port will be activated and where the content will be run. By using this method, you will be learning more about Docker and how you can build an image since you are doing everything on your own and it is not automated. The interactive method is also the place where you can troubleshoot an image should you be having an issue with it.

Method two

The other option that you have is to use the build method. If you like to use Docker files and all of the layers that it has to offer with Apache's server, then this is the method for you. Not only that, -but you will have site content that you can choose from the server which will save you a little bit of time so that you do not have to add a bunch of content that you find in someone else's template.

There will be a subdirectory that will be the best method that you can use as long as you give the subdirectory a name that is related to what you are doing, and you need to place them in the proper directory so that they can be found later on. You will also have the option of naming the files, it is recommended that you name them the same name as your directory so that you do not need to worry about selecting the wrong file.

With all of the content that is being used, you will find that it is easiest to copy it into a file so that you can move on to the next step and create the image so that it appears how you want it to. You need to remember that the ADD directive will need to be a new directory if you plan to use it.

A Docker file will have an httpd directory that will be based on the interactive method that was explained earlier. After you have created your directory, you can run it so that it looks at the image and ensures that it is the image that you want.

The container you use will have a process built into that will allow temporary images so that they can be layered and allow you to make the proper modifications. The number of layers you see will be reduced depending on the directives that are put into place.

Before you start, it is a good idea to plan out the layers you want so that you know how many you need to know how many to create when you are building the container.

Which method is the right method?

Whichever method you use will be based on why you are building the image. Every person will have their own reasons as to why they are creating the image or why they are using Docker which will ultimately factor into which method they will use. On top of that, you will need to choose your method based on which is easier for you to understand as you work through the steps.

Troubleshooting and prototyping

If you are having trouble and need to troubleshoot or prototype your image, you will most likely want to work with the first method. By using this technique, you will be receiving notes about the commands that you should be running. The commands will also be checked to see if they make sense or if there are files that need to be modified, removed, or transferred to a different container.

Satisfactory single build

If you are happy with a single image, then you should use method one that way the image can be reused in other projects in other areas of Docker. You will use the single file approach for every build that needs to take place in a single setting.

Managing images with Docker

After an image has been built and you are satisfied with it, you can share it with other Docker users. Your image that you create will be shared with others so that they can reuse the image in more ways that you would have ever been able to think of.

To share your image, it needs to be uploaded to the Docker hub. The hub will be a public registry the Docker developers maintain so that there are always images that can be reused by other members. There are well over fifteen thousand images that you will have access to on the Docker hub for your containers.

The Docker hub makes it possible for every user to work with tools that will improve their images workflow, privacy, and authenticity.

GitHub is similar to Docker's hub because it contains images that are built to be used specifically with Docker.

Here is how you can use begin using Docker hub.

Step one: create your account. Just like any other website that you create an account on, you need to input personal information and create a username and password that will allow you to access the images on the hub. The account that you create is going to be made by getting onto the Docker hub website and using the buttons on the homepage. Or, you can pull up your Docker command prompt and run the following command.

Syntax

$ Docker login

The login credentials that you make will be stored in a Docker folder on your server for the hub to remember you and the images that are linked to your username.

Command support

The web interface will enable you to search, push, or pull through a wide variety of repositories. The command will be one that you have used in other areas of Docker. You can find the command on the CLI of the Docker hub.

While you are doing your searching, you will use the name of the image, the person who created the image, or the description that was linked to the image when it was uploaded to Docker.

Push and pull commands will be used when you want to push or pull an image away from the hub.

Docker

Public repositories are open to everyone in the Docker community which means that everyone will have access to it. But, if you have an account, you will be using it when you use the push function. This is a special function for Docker hub members.

The image that you want to be placed on the hub will have to have a name, and it will have a container that will be named after that image. Therefore, name your images something memorable!

Chapter Three:

The Docker Orchestration

Linux has access to technology that uses kernels and makes it so that containerization is more accessible to all of its users as well as making it simpler to use. This will be similar to the orchestration that you see used with other containers.

Container orchestration will be used when you are transitioning between containers that have already been deployed by using a single host to those that use a more complex method when dealing with several container applications that are running through different machines. A distributed platform will be necessary so that it can be independent from the infrastructure that is going to be online the entire time that the application is running online. Your platform will end up assisting you to ensure that the application survives any failure that may occur because of an update to the software or a change in the hardware.

When dealing with the Docker orchestration, you will have two options. The first option will be to make an army of experts in technology that will be dealing with Docker and the ad hoc system that you are dealing with. But, the other option is to deal with a company that uses the same set of experts that will be used in setting up your Docker program and resolve any issues that arise. This will cost you, but you will be buying exclusively from the company and will have their support. When you use a company, it will be known as a lock-in when dealing with the modern world of technology.

Docker users will be required to decide which option they want to use, but these are not the best two options for everyone who is using the program. Because of this, Docker users pushed to have a third option that would include a platform created so that the orchestration could be used by all Docker users without having to deal with getting locked into a contract or wasting money that you may not have. Container orchestration will become easier to deal with when it is portable, faster, resilient, and secure.

There is an assortment of features that have been added to the core engine of Docker so that it can ensure the host works with several different containers which makes orchestration easier than it was with the previous versions of Docker. The newest API objects will manage and deploy applications that are in the engines; these applications are known as swarms. So, the best way to learn orchestration for Docker is to use Docker and figure it out yourself. You are bound to make a few mistakes, but you will get past them and be at an expert level in no time.

There are four main principles that Docker's orchestration design is based on.

1. Secure: security will be a default setting or Docker. The barriers that have been put in place for Docker are strong and have been given the proper certificates to

ensure that you can better understand PKI. PKI is used to remove the program. A few advanced users can control audits with certificates and the issuance that the program offers.

2. Features and backward compatibility: Docker has hundreds if not millions of users. To make sure that the program runs backward and is compatible with other programs is a major issue for the engine. This is why Docker is constantly updating to offer a better platform for its users.

3. Powerful and simple: orchestration is a major deal and is essential for the distribution of Docker applications. The orchestration will be a central part of the process that was first built into the core of Docker to allow it to follow the philosophy that has been listed in the Docker directory for a container to follow. You will only see a few small concepts that will be simple to learn but will make your experience with Docker better.

4. Resilient: computers and other pieces of technology are bound to fail at some point in time. There will be no way to stop the failure from stopping except to make the technology better. But, the program will be advanced enough that they can anticipate these failures and adapt without an application having to deal with the downtime that will follow the failure. That way when your machine fails, there will not be any damage done to your files.

Docker

Chapter Four:

Managing Swarms

With the latest version of Docker, you will have the opportunity to deal with a swarm on the Docker server.

Highlights

1. Decentralized design: the differentiation will end up handling what occurs between the roles that nodes will play when an application is deployed whenever the Docker engine is invoked at runtime. Both nodes will be deployed by a manager for the workers that are located in the Docker engine. This will allow you to create a swarm inside a single image.

2. Cluster management: the engine's CLI will be used when you are making swarms on the engine to allow you to deploy the service that an application will need. There will not be a need for any software that has been orchestrated when you are creating or managing swarms.

3. Declarative service models: the engine you use will use the approach that is declarative so that you can define the state of the service for your application.

4. Desired state reconciliation: the swarm manager will have to be monitored constantly so that any difference that occurs between the expressed desired state and the actual state of the nodes that need to be reconciled.

5. Scaling: every service that you use will have a number that will be declared for the tasks that you have already started. If you scale it up or down, then it will depend on the swarm manager, so it can adapt automatically to what is happening.

6. Multiple host network: there will be an overlay network that is specific to the services that are being used. The manager will have to assign the addresses of the containers on the network while it initializes or updates the applications that are being used.

7. Service discovery: the swarm manager node will have to assign every service that is used. Each swarm will contain a unique DNS name as well as a balanced load that will run a container through the server that has become embedded with the swarm.

8. Load balancing: you will have to expose the ports for the services that are being used outside of the program. Inside the program, you will have the option to distribute a container that will go between the nodes.

9. Rolling updates: there will be a few service updates that will have to be applied at the time of roll out so that the

nodes are incremented. The manager will allow you to have control of the delay that occurs between deployments of services that are set out for the nodes. If something happens, then you will be allowed to rewind the task to a version that came before so that you can fix any issues that may have occurred to get a different result.

10. Secure by default: a node will be enforced by a TLS authentication as well as an encryption that will ensure the communications are secure between nodes. You will not have the option of self-signing the certificates as a customer based on the CA root.

Mode key concepts

The cluster management will have some features that will be embedded in the engine that can be used with a swarm kit. The engines will work with the clusters that are located inside of the swarm's node. The node has to be enabled by the engine which will initialize the swarm; it may also add to the swarm that already exists in Docker.

Cluster shave to be deployed for the services in Docker. these services will require commands that are necessary for the swarm management. Some commands will be those that are used for adding and removing nodes. The CLI will come into play when the commands are used to manage Docker's orchestration.

The Docker engines will run outside of the swarm's node once the commands have been executed in a container.

Docker

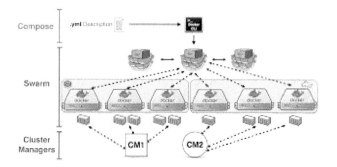

Chapter Five:

Networking

The Docker program will take care of most networking aspects for the containers to communicate with each other and the Docker host. If you use the ifconfig with your Docker host, then you will notice that the ethernet adapter for Docker will be created when Docker was installed on the Docker host. There will ultimately be a bridge that will link your Docker host to the Linux host.

Docker networks

To see all of the networks that are linked to the Docker host, you will use this command.

Syntax

Docker network ls

If there are no other options, then you will get a list of all the networks on the Docker host.

Example

Sudo Docker network ls

Docker

Inspecting a network in Docker

If you want to see more details about a network that is associated to Docker, you have to use the Docker network inspect command.

Syntax

Docker network inspect network name

Some of the options you will see are:

Network name: the name of the network the needs to be inspected

Your returned value will be the output of the details that can be located on the network.

Example

Sudo Docker network inspect bridge.

So, what would happen if you decide to run a container before you inspect the network? Take, for example, you want to place an Ubuntu container into the mix.

Example

Sudo Docker run -it ubuntu: latest / bin/ bash

Now, if you look at the name of the network from your command that was previously run, you will realize that the container has been attached to the bridge. After this, you will have the option of inspecting the bridge.

Example

Sudo Docker network inspect bridge

Creating your own network

When it comes to creating your own network, you have to do it before any containers can be launched.

Syntax

Docker network create - - driver driver name name

A few options you will have when it comes to creating a network.

Name the name the network has been given.

Driver name: the name that the driver name has been given.

The return you receive will be the network's long idea.

Example

Sudo Docker network creat - - driver bridge new _ nw

It is at this point that you will have the option of attaching your new network to the container that you are using.

Example

Sudo Docker run – it -network = new_ nw ubuntu : latest / bin / bash

Now, you will be inspecting your network with this command. You may notice that it will have a container attached to it.

Docker

Example

Sudo Docker network inspect new_nw

Chapter Six:

Building a Web Server

In this chapter, you gain the knowledge and skill set that you need to use a Docker file so that you can build a web server image. By building this image, you will have the option of building a container.

Step one: use VIM to build a Docker file

Example

From Ubuntu

Run apt – get update

Run apt – get install -y apache 2

Run apt – get install 0 y apache 2 -utils

Run apt – get clean

Expose 80 CMD [" apache 2 ctl" , -d foreground"]

You have to keep these things in mind about the code that you see above.

Docker

1. You will be creating an image from an image based on Ubuntu

2. The run command will be used to install Apache 2 on your image.

3. You will also use the run command to install the utility packages needed for Apache 2.

4. Next, the run command will be used to clean up files on the system.

5. The expose command will expose the 80th port in the Apache container on the Docker host.

6. The last command (CMD) will be used to run the Apache 2 command in the background while you work on other things

The details of the file will be entered so that all you need to do is save it.

Step two: run the build command so that the Docker file is built.

Syntax

sudo Docker build – t = "my web server"

You will not need to tag the image with the name of the image. Once the image is built, you will receive a message stating that the build is complete.

Step three: the web server file has to be built, and this can be completed by creating a second container. You will use the run command

Syntax

Sudo Docker run -d -p 80: 80 my web server

The port number will be exposed by the container numbered 80 and the -p command will assist in mapping to the 80th port on the local host.

The -d option will be used in running the container, so it is in a detached mode. This will ultimately end up sending the container into the background.

If you decide to go over to the 80th port, you will see that Apache will be what runs your web server.

Chapter Seven:

Setting Nodes. Js

Node.js will be the JavaScript framework you use when you develop a server sided application. This will be an open source framework that will be developed so that you can run several different operating systems. Since node.js is a popular framework for development, Docker can ensure that it supports all of JavaScripts applications.

In this section, you will get all of the steps listed out to follow them so that you can use a container for node.js and get it running.

Step one: you will need to pull an image from the hub. When you log into the Docker hub, you will be allowed to search for the image of node.js. All you will need to do is enter the node into the search box and select the node that comes up in the search results.

Step two: use the Docker pull command for the node you are working with. The details will be able to found in the repository which is located on the Docker hub.

Step three: while you are still on the Docker host, you will need to use the Docker pull command to download the latest node image from the hub. Once the pull has been completed, you will be allowed to proceed to the next step.

Step four: make sure that you are on the Docker host. You will need to use the VIM editor to ensure that you can create a node.js example file. This file will allow you to place the typical hello world command into the Docker prompt.

Example

Console.log ("hello world"):

The output you see will be "hello world" at your command prompt. However, to save the file, you have to go to step five.

Step five: make sure you are running the script properly. Use the node in the Docker container so that the following statement is executed.

Syntax

Sudo Docker run -ti -rm -name = hello world -v "$PWD":/ usr/src/app -w / usr / src / app node node hello world . js

You should know these two things about the syntax you just saw.

1. -rm: once a container has been run, it will be removed.

2. The container you use needs to be named hello world.

3. The volume needs to be mapped in the container by using /usr /src /app so that it can be linked to the present directory. After you have completed this, the

node container will select the script that is presently working with your directory on the Docker host.

4. -w: you will specify which directory is being used b node.js

5. The first node option will be used so that you can specify the node's image.

6. The second option that you have is to use the node that is running inside of the node container.

7. The last part of the script is the name.

The output that you see on the screen will be the node container that has been executed as you enter the code.

Chapter Eight:

Mongo DB

Mongo DB is considered to be one of the most famous document-oriented databases that will be used with a wide range of applications. Since the application is so popular, the database will be used for development; and Docker makes sure that it can support the database.

Here are the following steps that you have to follow to get Mongo DB up and running.

Step one: pull the image you want to use on the Docker hub. When you are locked in the hub, you will be searching to select the image that is on the hub for Mongo. All you will need to do is enter Mongo into the search box and choose the Mongo image that appears after your search results come up.

Step two: you will see the pull command for Docker in the details that you see listed in the repository.

Step three: Docker's host will use the pull command so that you can download the latest Mongo image.

Docker

Step four: now that you have the image, you will run a Mongo container that will allow you to have access to the instance for Mongo.

Syntax

Sudo Docker -it -d Mongo

Here is what you need to know about the code above.

1. Your container will be created by a Mongo image

2. -it: this will run the container in an interactive mode.

3. -d: your container will use the daemon process

You will need to issue the Docker ps command to see what containers are running inside the program.

Here are a few things that you should take note of:

1. The name of the container will be different and it has to keep changing since you will be using a spin container. But, you need to take note of the container that originally launched.

2. The port number that is running is important. You need to be using TCP port number 27017.

Step five: spin another container. This container will act like the client which will assist in connecting you to the Mongo database.

Syntax

Sudo Docker run -it -link = tender_ poitras: Mongo Mongo / bin / bash

Now you will be working with a new container.

Step six: the ENV command will be running inside the new container to allow you to locate the details on how to connect to the Mongo DB server container.

Step six: connect to the server with the client container by using this command.

Mongo 172. 17. 0. 2. 27017

You may notice that your IP and port numbers are what you received from the ENV command. The Mongo command will be your client command that will connect you to the Mongo database.

Once you have run the command, you will be able to run any command that you want inside your prompt.

Example

Use demo

By using this command, you will be allowed to switch to the database that is named demo. If the database is not available, then the program will be created for you.

You have now successfully created a server and a client that uses a Mongo DB container.

Docker

Chapter Nine:

Setting Up Docker NGINX

NGINX is a popular lightweight web application that you can use when you are developing a server-side application. Once again, it will be an open sourced web server that will be used in the development process, and Docker has made sure that it will support NGINX.

Now, let us examine the steps that you have to go through to get NGINX running on your Docker server.

Step one: pull your images from the Docker hub. When you log into Docker, you need to search for NGINX and select the first result that appears.

Step two: look at the details for the pull command which will be listed in the repository details.

Step three: the Docker host will use the pull command so that you can download the NGINX image.

Step four: run the NGINX container.

Syntax

Sudo Docker run -p 8080: 80 -d nginx

Docker

You may notice that you will be exposing the port for the NGINX server. The ports that you will be exposing are ports 80 through 808.

After you run the command, you should see something resembling this: http://Dockerhost:8080. This will show you the container is running as it should be.

Step five: once again you will be using the hello world command. If you do not want to use this command, you can use another command. However, the hello world one is the one that is commonly used so that you can understand what your code is doing in case you run into problems later.

Syntax

Sudo Docker run -p 8080: 80 -v "$pwd" :/ usr/ share/ nginx/ html: ro -d nginx

Points to notice about your code:

1. You will expose ports on the NGINX server these ports are 80 to 8080.

2. You have to attach the volume on the container to the directory that you are presently working on.

Once you have finished running the ode, you need to browse the URL HTTP:// Docker host: 8080/ hello world .HTML

If you used the hello world command, your output will be

Hello, world!

Chapter Ten:

Setting Up an ASP. Net

A SP. Net is a web development framework created by Microsoft for you to develop a server-side application. Since ASP. Net has been around for a long time, the Docker development team has made sure that Docker can support the application.

Some of the prerequisites for ASP. Net are:

1. You have to have a Windows system. Make sure that you are using Windows 10 or higher. You can always use Windows Server 2016.

2. Ensure that you have installed hyper-v and all of its containers on your Windows system. To install hyper-v, you need to go to your Windows features and enable them before making sure that the hyper-v option and containers button has been checked. You may find that you need to restart your system after you have finished this task to make sure that your changes have been applied.

3. You need to use the following command to ensure that you are installing the most updated version of Docker.

By using this command, you will be downloading and storing it in a temporary location.

Syntax

Invoke – web request "https:// test. Docker. Com / builds / windows/ x86_64/ Docker – 1. 13. 0 - . rc4. Zip" – use basic parsing.

4. Now expand the archive by using a PowerShell command.

Syntax

Expand – archive – path "$env: TEMP \ Docker – 1. 13. 0 -rc4. Zip" – destination path $env: program files

5. Use another PowerShell command to create a Docker file and enter it in the environment that you are currently working with.

Syntax

$env: path + = " ; $env: program files \ Docker"

6. Register the daemon service with another PowerShell command.

Syntax

Dockerd - - register – service

7. You need to start your daemon by using this command

Docker

Syntax

Start – service Docker

Being that you are using the Docker version of the command for PowerShell, you have to verify the daemon to ensure it is working correctly. Make sure you are being careful with the command or else you could end up getting another result.

Installing an ASP. Net container

Step one: find the image in Docker hub by researching Microsoft/ aspnet and clicking on the first image that appears.

Step two: you will see the pull command listed in the details for the repository so that you know exactly what is happening with the ASP.Net

Step four: copy and paste the following URL into your browser and download the whole GIT repository.

https://githut.com/microsoft/aspnet-Docker

step five: create a folder and name it application or app. Once it has been created, put it on your C drive. Copy all of the contents of 4.6.2/ sample folder into your C drive before moving to a Docker file and entering this command.

Syntax

Docker build -t aspnet – site – new – build -arg site_root = /

The code that you just used will have the following attributes.

1. The new image will be built and will be named aspnet – site – new

2. The root path will be placed in a local path folder.

Step six: run the container

Syntax

Docker run -d -p 8000: 80 – name my – running – site – ew aspnet – site – new

Step seven: Since the IIS is running in the Docker container, you will need to find your IP address that was used in the inspect command.

Chapter Eleven:

Kubernetecs Architecture

Kubernetecs is an orchestration framework that will work with a Docker container to expose the container as a service that works in the real world. For example, if you have two services, one will be the NGINX and the Mongo DB while the other service is NGINX and Redis. Every service will have an IP address or a service point that will help it connect to other applications. Kubernetecs will be used so that you can manage all of the services.

The minion mode will be where all of your services run. You will have a lot of minions that will run at the same time; but, remember that every minion will host multiple POD and each PODwill host a different set of containers. The proxy will be controlled by exposing the services in the outside world.

Every component for Kubernetecs will have a specific role.

1. ETCD: this will be the highly available key value that will store the service discoveries and any configurations that are shared. There will be a wide range of applications that connect the services to the discovery service.

2. Flannel: this is a black end network that has to be completed for a container to run properly.

3. Kube – API server: you will use this API for the orchestration of Docker containers.

4. Kube controller manager: you will use this so that you can control the Kuberntecs services.

5. Kube schedule: your containers will be scheduled on the Docker host.

6. Kubelet: this will be used in launching containers.

7. Kube – prox: this network will be provided through the proxy services to the outside world.

To install Kubentecs, you have to use kubeadm. This tool will aid you as you go through the installation process.

Step one: double check that the Ubuntu server is version 16.04 or higher.

Step two: generate an SSH key by using the SSH login. You can complete this task by using this command.

Syntax

Ssh – keygen

There will be a key generated in your home folder.

Step three: the next step will depend on what version of Ubuntu you are using. You will have to add a relevant site to the Docker list. This will work with the apt package manager

Docker

so that it can detect the Kubernetecs packages from the Kubernetecs site. It will also download them as they are supposed to.

Syntax

Curl – s https: // packages. Cloud. Gloogle. Com/ apt / doc/ apt – key. Gpg | apt – key – add – echo "deb httpe:// apt. Kubernetes. Io / kubernetes – xenial main" | sudo tee / etc / apt/ sources. List. d/ Docker. List

Step four: use the code to get an apt – get update so that you can ensure that all of your packages are downloaded on the server.

Step five: install the Docker package

Step six: install Kubernetecs

Syntax

Apt – get install – y kubelet kubadm kubectl kubernetes – cni

Step seven: once all the Kubernetecs packages are downloaded, you can begin using the Kubernetecs controller.

Syntax

Kubadm inti

Now that you have finished this step, you should receive a message that says all of the masters are up and running so now the nodes can join the clusters.

Chapter Twelve:

Cluster Deployment

Setting up a three node Kafka cluster

If you are using a Windows or Mach OS x, you will have to use a Docker machine so that the Docker host can be started. Docker will run natively on Linux systems. Therefore, the Docker host will be your local machine if you decide to go that route. However, if you are using Mac or Windows, you have to have at least four gigabytes of RAM for your Docker machine.

After all of your Docker dependencies have been installed, you need to create a Docker machine so that it can start the confluent platform.

Note: the steps below will run different Docker containers in a detached mode. But, you will see a demonstration on how you will need to access the logs in a container that is running. Should you prefer to run a container in the foreground, you can replace the -d in the code with - - it.

Step one: create and configure your Docker machine

Syntax

Docker – machine create - - driver virtualbox - - virtualbox – memory 6000 confluent

Now you have to configure your terminal window so it can be linked to your new Docker machine.

Syntax

Eval $ (Docker – machine env confluent)

Step two: start a three-node ZooKeeper Ensemble

Syntax

Docker run -d \

  --net=host \

  --name=zk-1 \

  -e ZOOKEEPER_SERVER_ID=1 \

  -e ZOOKEEPER_CLIENT_PORT=22181 \

  -e ZOOKEEPER_TICK_TIME=2000 \

  -e ZOOKEEPER_INIT_LIMIT=5 \

  -e ZOOKEEPER_SYNC_LIMIT=2 \

Docker

```
  -e
ZOOKEEPER_SERVERS="localhost:22888:23888;localhost:
32888:33888;localhost:42888:43888" \

  confluentinc/cp-zookeeper:4.0.0

Docker run -d \

  --net=host \

  --name=zk-2 \

  -e ZOOKEEPER_SERVER_ID=2 \

  -e ZOOKEEPER_CLIENT_PORT=32181 \

  -e ZOOKEEPER_TICK_TIME=2000 \

  -e ZOOKEEPER_INIT_LIMIT=5 \

  -e ZOOKEEPER_SYNC_LIMIT=2 \

  -e
ZOOKEEPER_SERVERS="localhost:22888:23888;localhost:
32888:33888;localhost:42888:43888" \

  confluentinc/cp-zookeeper:4.0.0

Docker run -d \

  --net=host \

  --name=zk-3 \

  -e ZOOKEEPER_SERVER_ID=3 \
```

-e ZOOKEEPER_CLIENT_PORT=42181 \

-e ZOOKEEPER_TICK_TIME=2000 \

-e ZOOKEEPER_INIT_LIMIT=5 \

-e ZOOKEEPER_SYNC_LIMIT=2 \

-e
ZOOKEEPER_SERVERS="localhost:22888:23888;localhost:
32888:33888;localhost:42888:43888" \

confluentinc/cp-zookeeper:4.0.0

Before you can go to the next step, you have to check the logs to make sure that the broker started properly. You can do this by running this command.

Syntax

Docker logs zk -1

By doing this, you should see this message at the end of your log.

Syntax

[2016-07-24 07:17:50,960] INFO Created server **with** tickTime 2000 minSessionTimeout 4000 maxSessionTimeout 40000 datadir /var/lib/zookeeper/log/version-2 snapdir /var/lib/zookeeper/data/version-2 (org.apache.zookeeper.server.ZooKeeperServer)

Docker

[2016-07-24 07:17:50,961] INFO FOLLOWING - LEADER ELECTION TOOK - 21823 (org.apache.zookeeper.server.quorum.Learner)

[2016-07-24 07:17:50,983] INFO Getting a diff **from** the leader 0x0 (org.apache.zookeeper.server.quorum.Learner)

[2016-07-24 07:17:50,986] INFO Snapshotting: 0x0 to /var/lib/zookeeper/data/version-2/snapshot.0 (org.apache.zookeeper.server.persistence.FileTxnSnapLog)

[2016-07-24 07:17:52,803] INFO Received connection request /127.0.0.1:50056 (org.apache.zookeeper.server.quorum.QuorumCnxManager)

[2016-07-24 07:17:52,806] INFO Notification: 1 (message format version), 3 (n.leader), 0x0 (n.zxid), 0x1 (n.round), LOOKING (n.state), 3 (n.sid), 0x0 (n.peerEpoch) FOLLOWING (my state) (org.apache.zookeeper.server.quorum.FastLeaderElection)

Here you can repeat your command for the other ZooKeeper nodes that you use. After that, you need to verify that your ZooKeeper ensemble is ready.

Syntax

for i in 22181 32181 42181; **do**

   Docker run --net=host --rm confluentinc/cp-zookeeper:4.0.0 bash -c "echo stat | nc localhost $i | grep Mode"

done

You should see a single leader node and two follower nodes. Now, your output should look like this.

Syntax

Mode: follower

Mode: leader

Mode: follower

Step three: ZooKeeper should now be running, and this will cause the three nodes to start in the Kafka cluster.

Syntax

Docker run -d \

  --net=host \

  --name=kafka-1 \

  -e
KAFKA_ZOOKEEPER_CONNECT=localhost:22181,localhost:32181,localhost:42181 \

  -e
KAFKA_ADVERTISED_LISTENERS=PLAINTEXT://localhost:29092 \

  confluentinc/cp-kafka:4.0.0

Docker run -d \

Docker

```
  --net=host \

  --name=kafka-2 \

  -e
KAFKA_ZOOKEEPER_CONNECT=localhost:22181,localhost:
32181,localhost:42181 \

  -e
KAFKA_ADVERTISED_LISTENERS=PLAINTEXT://localho
st:39092 \

  confluentinc/cp-kafka:4.0.0

Docker run -d \

  --net=host \

  --name=kafka-3 \

  -e
KAFKA_ZOOKEEPER_CONNECT=localhost:22181,localhost:
32181,localhost:42181 \

  -e
KAFKA_ADVERTISED_LISTENERS=PLAINTEXT://localho
st:49092 \

  confluentinc/cp-kafka:4.0.0
```

Be sure to check your logs to see if your broker has started
properly!

```
Docker logs kafka-1
```

Docker logs kafka-2

Docker logs kafka-3

You should see this message for your bootup message pertaining to this command.

Syntax

Docker logs Kafka – 3 | grep started

Your output should be

Syntax

[2016-07-24 07:29:20,258] INFO [Kafka Server 1003], started (kafka.server.KafkaServer)

[2016-07-24 07:29:20,258] INFO [Kafka Server 1003], started (kafka.server.KafkaServer)

As soon as your broker begins to act as a controller, you should begin to see a message similar to this.

Syntax

[2016-07-24 07:29:20,283] TRACE Controller 1001 epoch 1 received response {error_code=0} **for** a request sent to broker localhost:29092 (id: 1001 rack: null) (state.change.logger)

[2016-07-24 07:29:20,283] TRACE Controller 1001 epoch 1 received response {error_code=0} **for** a request sent to broker localhost:29092 (id: 1001 rack: null) (state.change.logger)

Docker

```
[2016-07-24 07:29:20,286] INFO [Controller-1001-to-broker-
1003-send-thread], Starting
(kafka.controller.RequestSendThread)

[2016-07-24 07:29:20,286] INFO [Controller-1001-to-broker-
1003-send-thread], Starting
(kafka.controller.RequestSendThread)

[2016-07-24 07:29:20,286] INFO [Controller-1001-to-broker-
1003-send-thread], Starting
(kafka.controller.RequestSendThread)

[2016-07-24 07:29:20,287] INFO [Controller-1001-to-broker-
1003-send-thread],    Controller    1001    connected    to
localhost:49092 (id: 1003 rack: null) for sending state change
requests (kafka.controller.RequestSendThread)
```

Step four: test the broker to make sure it is working.

With the brokers now up, you need to test them to make sure they are working. You will do this by creating a topic.

Syntax

```
Docker run \

  --net=host \

  --rm \

  confluentinc/cp-kafka:4.0.0 \

  kafka-topics --create --topic bar --partitions 3 --replication-
factor 3 --if-not-exists --zookeeper localhost:32181
```

You will get the following result.

Created topic "bar".

Here you will verify that your topic has been created by describing the topic.

Syntax

Docker run \

  --net=host \

  --rm \

  confluentinc/cp-kafka:4.0.0 \

  kafka-topics   --describe   --topic   bar   --zookeeper localhost:32181

In the terminal window, you will see this result.

Syntax

Topic:bar   PartitionCount:3   ReplicationFactor:3 Configs:

Topic: bar Partition: 0 Leader: 1003   Replicas: 1003,1002,1001   Isr: 1003,1002,1001

Topic: bar Partition: 1 Leader: 1001   Replicas: 1001,1003,1002   Isr: 1001,1003,1002

Topic: bar Partition: 2 Leader: 1002   Replicas: 1002,1001,1003   Isr: 1002,1001,1003

Docker

After that is done, you need to try and generate some data by using the bar topic that was just created.

Syntax

Docker run \

 --net=host \

 --rm confluentinc/cp-kafka:4.0.0 \

 bash -c "seq 42 | kafka-console-producer --broker-list localhost:29092 --topic bar && echo 'Produced 42 messages.'"

The command that you just put into the command prompt will pass 42 integers while you use the Console Producer that is shipped with Kafka. Because of this, you will see something similar to this:

Syntax

Produced 42 messages

It will appear that everything is written successfully, however, you should read the messages back by using the Console Consumer and ensuring that everything is accounted for.

Syntax

Docker run \

--net=host \

--rm \

confluentinc/cp-kafka:4.0.0 \

kafka-console-consumer --bootstrap-server localhost:29092 --topic bar --new-consumer --from-beginning --max-messages 42

After some time, you will see this output. Kafka will have created this output by using the _consumers _offset topic behind the working program so that you can work with data for the first time. Do not be surprised if this takes a long time to process.

Syntax

1

4

7

10

13

16

....

41

Processed a total of 42 messages

Setting up a three node Kafka cluster

Install Docker and Docker compose before you start this section. After you have done that, you will follow these steps to start your Confluent Platform services.

Docker

Step one: Clone your Confluent Platform Docker images in the Github Repository

Syntax

git clone `https://github.com/confluentinc/cp-Docker-images`

You will have a Docker Compose file that will start ZooKeeper and Kafka. You have to navigate to

Syntax

Cp – Docker – images / examples /kafka -cluster

Start two: start ZooKeeper and Kafka with Docker Compose's 'up' command

Syntax

Docker – compose up

Your result should be displayed as you see below.

Syntax

Name	Command	State	Ports
kafkacluster_kafka-1_1	/etc/confluent/Docker/run	Up	
kafkacluster_kafka-2_1	/etc/confluent/Docker/run	Up	
kafkacluster_kafka-3_1	/etc/confluent/Docker/run	Up	

kafkacluster_zookeeper-1_1 /etc/confluent/Docker/run Up

kafkacluster_zookeeper-2_1 /etc/confluent/Docker/run Up

kafkacluster_zookeeper-3_1 /etc/confluent/Docker/run Up

Besure to check the ZooKeeper log to make sure that it is healthy.

Syntax

Docker-compose logs zookeeper-1

Your result will be as follows

Syntax

zookeeper-1_1 | [2016-07-25 04:58:12,901] INFO Created server with tickTime 2000 minSessionTimeout 4000 maxSessionTimeout 40000 datadir /var/lib/zookeeper/log/version-2 snapdir /var/lib/zookeeper/data/version-2 (org.apache.zookeeper.server.ZooKeeperServer)

zookeeper-1_1 | [2016-07-25 04:58:12,902] INFO FOLLOWING - LEADER ELECTION TOOK - 235 (org.apache.zookeeper.server.quorum.Learner)

Verify that your ZooKeeper ensemble is prepared to be used.

for i in 22181 32181 42181; **do**

   Docker run --net=host --rm confluentinc/cp-zookeeper:4.0.0 bash -c "echo stat | nc localhost $i | grep Mode"

Docker

done

From here you will see a single leader and two followers

Syntax

Mode: follower

Mode: leader

Mode: follower

Go back to the locks to make sure that broker has been booted up successfully.

Syntax

Docker-compose logs kafka-1

Docker-compose logs kafka-2

Docker-compose logs kafka-3

The following message should this bootup message

Syntax

kafka-3_1 | [2016-07-25 04:58:15,189] INFO [Kafka Server 3], started (kafka.server.KafkaServer)

kafka-3_1 | [2016-07-25 04:58:15,189] INFO [Kafka Server 3], started (kafka.server.KafkaServer)

Whenever your broker begins acting like a controller, you will see this message.

Syntax

kafka-3_1 | [2016-07-25 04:58:15,369] INFO [Controller-3-to-broker-2-send-thread], Controller 3 connected to localhost:29092 (id: 2 rack: null) **for** sending state change requests (kafka.controller.RequestSendThread)

kafka-3_1 | [2016-07-25 04:58:15,369] INFO [Controller-3-to-broker-2-send-thread], Controller 3 connected to localhost:29092 (id: 2 rack: null) **for** sending state change requests (kafka.controller.RequestSendThread)

kafka-3_1 | [2016-07-25 04:58:15,369] INFO [Controller-3-to-broker-1-send-thread], Controller 3 connected to localhost:19092 (id: 1 rack: null) **for** sending state change requests (kafka.controller.RequestSendThread)

kafka-3_1 | [2016-07-25 04:58:15,369] INFO [Controller-3-to-broker-1-send-thread], Controller 3 connected to localhost:19092 (id: 1 rack: null) **for** sending state change requests (kafka.controller.RequestSendThread)

kafka-3_1 | [2016-07-25 04:58:15,369] INFO [Controller-3-to-broker-1-send-thread], Controller 3 connected to localhost:19092 (id: 1 rack: null) **for** sending state change requests (kafka.controller.RequestSendThread)

Note: using Docker – compose log| grep controller will make it easier for you to grep through all of your logs for all of your services.

Conclusion

Thank you for making it through to the end of *Docker*, let's hope it was informative and able to provide you with all of the tools you need to achieve your goals whatever it may be.

The next step is to use the advanced strategies that you learned in this book so that you can control Docker better. By using the information that you learned in this book, you will learn the strategies that you need so that you no longer are limited in what you can do with Docker.

There was a lot of code in this book that may have made your head spin, but do not let that stop you from using Docker. When you understand the code in Docker, you will have the option of moving on to programming languages that are more complex. Not to mention, you can use other programming languages in Docker to manipulate your Docker images.

There is always more that you will be able to learn about using Docker and I am glad that you picked up this book to help you on your journey. Hopefully, you were able to learn more about Docker so that you no longer have any questions about Docker.

Remember, if you have questions about Docker, you can always find the answer on the Docker website!

Finally, if you found this book useful in any way, a review on Amazon is always appreciated!

Thank you and good luck using Docker!